DISMANTLING THE STRONGHOLD OF DEPRESSION

21 DAYS OF PRAYER

LATOYA CHRISTMAN

Cover Design: Joy Osborne

Dedication

I dedicate this prayer book to my mother Carol Lynette Fields. When I thought about this book, the first person I thought of was you. You are a true overcomer. No matter what problems or issues arise, you are a fighter and a person who prevails. Depression will not have its way in your life. My prayer is this journal will not only save your life but will also free many others from the stronghold of depression. I thank God for your life, and I want you to know that the heartache and pain you endured was not in vain. I love you and may God bless your life, Mom.

Love, Latoya

Acknowledgements

I would like to first take the time to acknowledge my Heavenly Father who has been my all and everything. Through the ups and the downs and turn arounds, God has proven Himself to still be God in my life. I give Him praise, glory, and honor for what He continues to do in my life.

I would like to acknowledge my amazing daughter, Madisen Denise. Words can never express how much you mean to me. You are my heart. You are my everything. You have been my reason for pushing through. You're such a loving, kind, gentle spirit. You love me despite my flaws. You have stuck things out with me through the hard times, the ups, and the downs. You are truly an anointed vessel. Words can never express how proud I am to call you my daughter I pray God will continue to bless you and keep you all the days of your life. I love you so much, Madisen Denise. Mommy is so proud of you!

Thank you to my mother and my father, Carol Fields and Benny Christman, for coming together and giving birth and life to me. If it had not been for you guys, I would not even be here. I thank you for your prayers, your love, and your support as I go through this journey in ministry, as a mother, and one day a wife. I love you guys dearly and I continue to keep you close in my heart and in my prayers.

Thank you to my siblings, Charima, Betty, Tyran, Marte, and Benny, Jr. for your love, support, jokes and constantly giving me a reason to stay on my knees praying. I love you guys tremendously and pray for nothing but the best for you. Thank you to my family near and far in California for your prayers, your love, and support as well. To my very own Apostle Shante Ligons and Rebirth Apostolic Ministries family, words can never express how much you guys truly mean to me. Apostle, you were my saving grace during a time in my life when I was dying spiritually. I love you, Apostle, for your prayers, your continuous sacrifice, and support. I truly know the heart posture of a leader and I have learned so much while being under your leadership. You have been an example of loving people unconditionally and you literally have saved my life. If you feel as if you have never done anything in this world or made a difference, just know you have saved a nation of people just through me. I thank you for all that you continue to do.

Rebirth Nation, we do it better together.

Foreword

As I have watched the growth and the rapid maturity of Pastor Latoya, it is, indeed, befitting and a great charge that The Father would use her to impart such a display of love through this book. The topic of depression is an unchartered area, often missed based on the fact that people look at outer appearances, missing the signs of someone that is wounded and crying out for help on the inside. This devotional will give hope to the hopeless, encouragement to the lost, and the strength that is needed to go on through the power of prayer. I say to every person that reads this 21 Day Devotional that you are not alone. Pastor Latoya has taken the liberty of including real testimonials for transparency and to disclose the raw truth of life, as well as praise breaks that give the assurance that you will break this stronghold. Every person who encounters this book will be changed forever. I am so honored to have had a front row seat on this journey. As your Apostle, I see you plowing, doing what you have been created to do. Thank you for your labor of love for the people, and exposing the plot of the enemy that this book will annihilate because of your posture.

— *Apostle Shantay Ligons*

Introduction

Merriam Dictionary defines depression as a mood disorder characterized by varying degrees of sadness, despair, and loneliness. Depression is typically accompanied by inactivity, guilt, loss of concentration, social withdrawal, sleep disturbances, and sometimes suicidal tendencies. 19.4 million Americans have dealt with at least one major depressive episode in their lives. Depression has killed destiny, dreams, purpose, families, marriages, relationships, churches, leadership and so much more. Some argue that depression is not a stronghold but simply a mental disorder that cannot be overcome.

Some believe medication is the only treatment and there is not enough prayer in the world to rid a person of depression. This is untrue. With prayer, deliverance, God's word, and a support system (family, counselors, clergy, etc.), can allow a person to experience true freedom. Depression is usually caused by trauma, an emotional disturbance, or a sudden loss. Of course, these are NOT the only reasons for depression but rather a few examples of the origin of depression.

These daily prayers are a way to speak something into existence that currently is not in operation. Each prayer can be used to dismantle depression in day-to-day life. The purpose of each prayer point is to realign your life and unlock deliverance. Every life experience plays a significant role in how we think and how we act. I pray this prayer book will help guide every reader to freedom and restoration.

The Plan of Salvation

There will be many who will come across these prayers and their lives will be changed forever. It is my desire for each of you reading this book to know your identity in God and solidify your salvation. There is comfort in knowing that you are saved. If you were to leave this earth today or tomorrow, do you know where you would lift your eyes? I offer the plan of salvation to those of you who are unsure of your salvation. In John 3:16, it says, "For God so loved the world that He gave his only begotten Son, that whoever believes in him should not perish but have everlasting life." In John 10:10 Jesus declared, "I have come that they may have life, and that they may have it more abundantly." Romans 3:23 reveals, "all have sinned and fallen short of the glory of God." Romans 6:23 discloses, "For the wages of sin is death; but the gift of God *is* eternal life in Christ Jesus our Lord." Romans 5:8 declares, "But God demonstrates his own love towards us in this: While we were still sinners, Christ died for us." This scripture is evidence of redemption and God's love towards us. If you desire to be saved, say the following: *"I repent of my sins. I confess with my mouth the Lord Jesus, and I believe in my heart that God has raised Jesus from the dead. I believe Jesus Christ died on the cross for my sins and rose on the third day. For with the heart one believes unto righteousness, and with the mouth confession is made unto salvation. Whoever calls on the name of the Lord shall be saved."* Through the confession of your faith, you are now saved.

Welcome to Sonship!

Sonship is a term that refers to the status of being a son or daughter of God. It is not a natural or literal relationship, but a spiritual and metaphoric one. Sonship implies that believers have been adopted into God's family and can call him Father. It also means that they have the same nature and rights as God's Son, Jesus Christ, who is the perfect example of sonship. Sonship involves having a heart of obedience and submission to God and his leaders.

Table of Contents

Prayer 1: Five Senses

Prayer 2: The Heart

Prayer 3: Offense

Prayer 4: Rejection

Prayer 5: Identity

Prayer 6: The Mind

Prayer 7: Premature Death

Breakthrough – Allison Foster

Prayer 8: Abandonment

Prayer 9: Abuse

Prayer 10: Addictions

Prayer 11: Trauma

Prayer 12: Shame

Prayer 13: Angry

Prayer 14: Pride

Breakthrough – Carol Fields

Prayer 15: Perversion

Prayer 16: Self-Sabotage

Prayer 17: Finances

Prayer 18: Ministry

Prayer 19: Anxiety

Prayer 20: Suicidal Thoughts

Prayer 21: Depression

Breakthrough – Minister Latoya Christman

-1-

The Five Senses

Heavenly Father, I thank you right now for what you continuously do through my senses. I thank you, God, for my ability to use all five senses to discern what the spirit and word of God is saying. I do not take for granted your power and the anointing that you have given me through taste, touch, hearing, smell, and sight in order to be used as a vessel in the earth. Thank you that according to your word in Psalms 34:8 where it says, "Taste and see that the Lord is good: blessed is the one who takes refuge in him." I trust that what God has placed inside of me from the creation of mankind has been opened through my senses. I thank you that the lust of the flesh, lust of the eyes, and the pride of life comes NOT from the Father but from the world according to 1 John 2:16 and as a result we are to live a life of holiness. I thank you God for giving me the ability to watch and pray so that I may not fall into temptation according to what your word says in Matthew 26:41. I thank you Lord that my touch is as soft as your love for me and that my taste is as sweet as the Holy Spirit. I thank you God that my eyesight is as clear as an eagle and my hearing is submitted to your voice as your son Jesus was to you. I decree and declare that I will no longer be blindsided by the enemy and that you have opened my eyes to be able to see the things to which I was once naive. I thank you God that through my hearing I will be able to comprehend the things that I was once ignorant to, and you are bringing about clarity in my life. I decree and declare I will no longer walk closed minded and now trust in my senses in Jesus' name. Amen.

Praise Break

We show little appreciation on a day-to-day basis for the five senses. They are truly a blessing from God. When I hear people say they do not know the difference between their voice and the voice of God, I know they lack the ability to hear from a sound mind. Thank God for a sound mind. Confusion will step in when we are fearful of what God is showing us. God has not given us a spirit of fear but of power, love, and a sound mind. (2 Timothy 1:7)

When we do not want to see what God is showing us, we start neglecting our five senses, and our spiritual vision becomes blurred. I thank God for clear vision! Hinderances and blockages occur when we do not let go and let God. It is necessary for us to be open to God's revelation and insight to heal on this journey.

Over the years using my senses could have kept me out of troublesome situations. For example, I allowed the lust of the eyes to lead me into toxic relationships. My desire to taste overruled the voice of God. There is healing in admitting that I knew better. There is redemption in confessing that I heard God say "No" and did it anyway. Thank God for the five senses! I praise God for the warnings before destruction because now I can look back and tell others the importance of using their senses. The longer I stayed, the harder it was to come out. Although I could see that this relationship was pulling life out of me, causing me to feel defeated and depressed, I stayed anyway. I felt like the work that it would take to get out was too much to bear. As a result, it continued to cause pain and turmoil that led to a place of depression and oppression. This is a reminder that God does not put any more on us than we can bear. I came out. You can come out, too.

It is important to pray for God to heal our perspective. I am grateful that God healed my perspective because my perspective is my reality. That is what I wake up to each morning. Now that I am able to see God's vision for my life, the spirit of depression cannot bind me. I follow Him because I can see that His ways are better than my ways. I praise God for discernment because I can hear His voice. I can proclaim that He is, indeed, good because I have tasted His grace and mercy. I love the scent of being in His presence. My meditation of Him is sweet. I am glad in the Lord. (Psalm 104:34) Just like the woman who touched the helm of Jesus' garment, I am healed. I am free. I am delivered! To God be the Glory!

Reflections

-2-

The Heart

Heavenly Father, I come to you as humbly as I know how asking you, Father, to come into this heart of flesh and consume everything that is not like you. My heart is hurt and damaged and I am tired. God, I want to love but do not know how. I need your help. Father I believe by the power of the Holy Spirit that you can heal the broken-hearted. According to the word in Psalms 147:3, you "heal the broken hearted and bandage their wounds." Father, I believe by your word my heart is being healed and the wounds on the inside of me are now being filled by the power and the anointing of the Holy Spirit. I thank you that I now walk in a new heart and the old heart is no more. I thank you for this new heart to serve, to love unconditionally without any limits or restrictions. I thank you that this is a heart that operates through the gifts of the spirit and the fruits of the spirit. I thank you that my heart radiates with compassion and love for your people. I thank you now God that my heart no longer has residue of bitterness, rejection, anger or even offense. For it says in Proverbs 14:30 "a heart at peace gives life to the body but envy rots the bones." I am glad that my heart is happy, and my face is cheerful. I submit this new heart to you. Do what you please, Lord, and I believe that it will be satisfying unto you. I open my heart unto thee. By faith I now walk in a clean, healed, and pure heart that is holy and acceptable unto you in Jesus' name. Amen.

Praise Break

Thank God that the heart is a muscle. With muscles, the longer you work on them, the stronger they get. Over the years, I have been careless with my heart and the heart is the gateway to the soul. When the gatekeeper is not at his post, anyone can enter. When you neglect a muscle, it will atrophy and become weak. When my heart was weak, I made some mistakes but praise God, we are not the sum of our mistakes. We are who He says we are. We are fearfully and wonderfully made. (Psalm 139:14)

Even the most luxurious cars require maintenance. We are the same way. There is nothing wrong with God's craftmanship. He created us in His own image, but we have to maintain our hearts, minds, bodies, and souls. When life starts giving us trouble, we have to check the owner's manual – His holy word. Thank God for always giving us everything we need!

You may be at a point in your life where you are making decisions that are not in the will of God. I have been there. The exciting thing about repentance is you can choose it any time. God meets us at our point of need. That is the reason I cannot help but praise Him. I have been right where you are and as I matured in faith, I began to heal and make better decisions. The word of God instructs us to hide His word in our hearts. (Psalm 119:11) The more Word I put into my heart, the stronger my heart got because there was less room for the things that led to the depression. The healing started with simply surrendering to God.

After enduring cycles of repeated trauma, my heart was broken, but the thing about muscles is with a little care, they spontaneously regenerate themselves! Life says I am defeated, but God said victory is mine! Life says I am depressed, but God said no weaponed formed against me would prosper. Life says the situation is hopeless, but God said because I have Him my heart is glad, and my glory rejoices; my flesh shall rest in hope! Life says I should be angry, but the joy of the Lord is my strength!

Reflections

-3-

Offense

Heavenly Father, offense has crippled my heart, my mind, and my spirit from the beginning of time. Offense has killed my dreams, my visions, and even my perspective on life. Father, I am tired of the cycles of offense. Today I declare that by your stripes I am healed from offense. I will no longer allow offense to cripple my heart, my mind and my spirit which causes my dreams, my visions, praise, worship, and even my perspective on life to die. I believe and trust that through your word, Father, my family, and everyone assigned to my destiny is set free from the shackles of offense. Good sense makes one slow to anger and it is your glory to overlook an offense according to Proverbs 19:11. I trust that you are leading me to this place of intimacy with you, Father God. I trust the Holy Spirit to intercede on behalf of something that seems bigger than you. I ask you, Father, to give me the strength to forgive those who have offended me and even the moments when I have been the offender. Oh, Father, continue to reveal any unresolved issues in my heart that I choose to not let go of because of the spirit of offense. I choose to relinquish on this day every past relationship that ended prematurely due to offense. I renounce bitterness and a hardened heart due to offense. I give up the right to isolate myself from people and places that offended me, and I stand boldly and confident in who I am. Give me wisdom and insight on how to respond to situations and circumstances that may cause me to go into a place of being offended. Increase my discernment to see things through the lens of Christ and the Holy Spirit. Thank you, God, for your unfailing love towards me while

I was yet a sinner. Thank you, God, that I am no longer a victim but a survivor. I believe by faith I am set free, healed, and delivered in Jesus' name. Amen.

Praise Break

The truth is no one likes to feel offended, and no one likes to feel like they are being exposed, embarrassed, or even left vulnerable but by his stripes we are set free from being offended. What the enemy meant for bad God has turned it around for our good. I. too, was a person who dealt with offense in different areas of my life. God began to heal the areas that were unhealed and wounded when I learned about His sovereign love and Sonship, my identity in Him. I know that He will heal you, too.

In order to be free God must get the glory in our lives. I tell my clients in counseling that healing is like a wound with a deep infection. When a doctor treats a wound, they get out the infection, clean the area really good, apply the medication for healing, stitch it up, and apply a bandage. Despite the situation that occurred to cause the wound (the offense), despite the pain the patient endured during the removal of the infection (anger, unforgiveness, plots of revenge), despite the discomfort of the extensive cleansing (repentance, turning it over to God), when the doctor (God) put that medication (peace) on that wound for healing, when the doctor (God) stitched it up (deliverance) and when that bandage was applied and that wound was covered (in the blood of Jesus, the patient could rest knowing that everything would be fine. When there's a doctor in the room, a patient has an assurance that healing can take place.

God is the doctor in the room when we are overcoming offense. He is the doctor that we need to treat the pain. I give him all the honor and praise for showing up for me time and time again. To be set free from the stronghold of offense, I had to see Dr. Jesus. You need to make an appointment with Him, too.

Reflections

-4-

Rejection

Heavenly Father, I come to you thanking you for who you are and your loving kindness towards me. I thank you that I am no longer a slave to rejection. I decree and declare, Father God, that you have severed every illegal contract that tied me to rejection. I thank God that I am set free and delivered. My emotions are free from the past hurt of rejection. The trauma I experienced as a result of rejection is a vehicle to my destiny. I will no longer associate rejection by people with my identity in God. Rejection is a steppingstone to spiritual wealth and prosperity in the natural world. I thank God that I am no longer consumed by the negative opinions of others, or the word curses they spoke over my life. I thank God that what the enemy meant for bad, God is turning it around for my good. I bind the hand of the enemy that tries to remind me of the rejection and trauma I experienced in my childhood. God, you are erasing every memory that causes me to revert into a place of feeling rejected. I thank God that the suffering I experienced identified me as a child of the highest God and not as an orphan. The suffering was necessary. Isaiah 53:3 is an example of what your son endured. He was despised and rejected by mankind, a man of suffering, and familiar with pain. Like one from whom people hide their faces, he was despised, and we held him in low esteem. I praise God and I lift you up and I magnify you for keeping me despite the moments when I felt I could not be kept. I thank you, God, that during my moments of rejection, you sustained me. I kept the faith like your son Abraham and by faith, I obtained freedom and healing. Today is the day I walk in it which is so freely given in Jesus' name. Amen.

Praise Break

Overcoming rejection reminds me of the story of Mephibosheth in the Bible. Mephibosheth was the son of Jonathan and grandson of Saul. His story is found in first and second Samuel. Mephibosheth became crippled and lame from being dropped by his nanny. As a result, he was rejected and hidden from society.

That could have been the end of Mephibosheth's story – Bud God! God used David to bless Mephibosheth through a promise that David made to Jonathan. David promised to take care of Mephibosheth for the rest of his life, and he fulfilled that promise. What could have been a lifetime of rejection, God turned into a place at the king's table of royalty. When we feel cast out and rejected, God send someone to be a blessing during our healing process.

Society will tell us we are too short, too tall, too fat, too thin, too dark, too light, too religious, not religious enough, etc. The enemy will use the stronghold of rejection to make us second guess God and the gifts He has given us. The enemy has come to kill (our confidence), steal (our self-esteem), and destroy (our purpose). His goal is to make God reject us when our life's journey is over. The good news is we do not have to worry about the judgement of society, and we have victory over the plans of the enemy. This battle is already won. We are beautifully and wonderfully made.

Rejection can be painful but there is purpose in the pain. God wants to use the rejection to direct us to a place of joy, peace, and abundance in Him. That's why we should praise Him in the midst of rejection, knowing He has already worked it out for our good, just like

He did for Mephibosheth. To God be the glory for the things He has done!

Reflections

-5-

Identity

Father God, I thank you that my identity is not determined by man, but my identity is matched with Genesis 2 :7 which states "then the Lord God formed the man from the dust of the ground, he breathed the breath of life into the man's nostrils and the man became a living person." I thank you that through your breath I'm able to breathe and have a new life. I thank God that according to Genesis 1:27 you created humans in your image in the image of God you created us male and female. Which means our identity is in you. You have given me dominion and authority over the earth and that makes my heart glad. I decree and declare the word of God spoken over my life and the revelation of your word will always abide in my heart and mind. I do not have to conform to the things of this world, and I do not have to search for acceptance from people. You have made me as my own unique self and for this I give God the glory and honor. The only desire I have is to be accepted by you, God, and that my life mirrors a true reflection of who you are. I thank you that I am a royal priesthood, a chosen race, a holy nation, a people for your possession according to 1 Peter 2:9. I thank God that according to 2 Corinthians 5:17 that "if anyone is in Christ, he is a new creation. The old has passed away; behold, the new has come." The new me has come forward and I am solidified in Christ Jesus. I bind the hand of the enemy that seeks to deceive me through feelings, emotions, thoughts, deception, and manipulation. I close every door and entry point that causes me to go backwards into the divers' temptations and compromise my identity. I come against every word curse spoken over my identity and my blood line. I no longer come into agreement with the spirit of confusion, irritation, and frustration because I have the mind of Christ. I throw off everything that hinders and the sin that so easily entangles. And I run with perseverance the race marked out for me fixing my eyes on Jesus, the pioneer and perfecter of faith according to Hebrews 12:1-2 in Jesus' name. Amen.

Praise Break

When I hear the term identity crisis, a state of emergency comes to mind; one that needs immediate attention and requires the biggest sergeant to take charge. The only sergeant that can handle the job is Christ Jesus. I have learned through personal experiences that an identity crisis is often a cry for help. There is something on the inside yearning for someone or something that is safe. There is a void.

The best way to fill a void in our life is with Jesus. His presence in our lives solidifies our identity in Him. We are who he says we are. The greatest gift in the world is knowing that God gave his only son Christ so that we may live. We are now free to walk in Sonship. This relationship comes with saving redemption and God's everlasting love. God loves with no reservation. He is not looking for perfection. God knows our struggles. He knows our hidden places that need healing..

The world likes to put limitations on what God can do and who he can use to draw the people to Christ, but I know a God who has no limitations. Even if identity crisis has been your battle, I want to introduce you to God who will heal, restore, and bring wholeness to you. He is a God who wraps his loving arms around you and whispers how great of a God he is. You can trust him. He sends out his angels to surround, encamp, and keep you when you are overcome with emptiness, loneliness, and rejection..

Rejoice because no weapon formed against you shall prosper. You can stand on the promises of God. What the enemy meant for bad, God is turning it around for your good.

Reflections

-6-

The Mind

Father God, I bind the strong man of defeat, confusion, manipulation, arrested development, schizophrenia, self-sabotage, and every tormenting spirit that seeks to control my mind. I reclaim back my mind and dismantle every though that exalts itself against the knowledge of Christ. I capture every thought and overthrow reasonings and lead captive every thought into the obedience of Christ According to 2 Corinthians 10:5. I will not rehearse the same thoughts that lead me into a place of depression, insecurity, doubt, fear, or anxiety. I decree and declare I will fix my thoughts on what is true, honorable, right, pure, lovely, and admirable according to Philippians 4:8. My mind will no longer be bound by a poverty mindset. I will occupy my mind with things that are beneficial to my future. I will not only obtain spiritual wealth but also wealth in the natural. I am walking into my blessings because I believe through the Holy Spirit I can do so. My mind will supersede my expectations because I have the mind of Christ. I put on the helmet of salvation and renew my mind daily according to Romans 12:1-2. My mind will not continue to wander into places that will cause my dreams to die. I have the power to shut down every perverted thought that will cause separation from you. I thank you, God. I know you as the Prince of Peace, according to Isaiah 9:6. For a child is born to us, a son is given to us. The government will rest on his shoulders. And he will be called: Wonderful Counselor, Mighty God, Everlasting Father, Prince of Peace. I believe by faith that we can have peace with God according to Isaiah 53:5. It is evidence the Holy Spirit is working in my life, and I receive it according to Galatians 5:22. I thank you God that through my prayer life I will continue to have peace because your word says in Philippians 4:4-7 that we can have peace through prayer. I commit myself to a lifestyle of prayer, consecration and fasting. I understand the renewing of the mind takes time and I am committed to the process. I will be patient with myself, I will not look at what I see and forget the promises made in my life. I choose peace, love, happiness, and joy. My mind is set on things which are above and not beneath. I look forward - forgetting those things which are behind me. I decree and declare I have freedom in Christ Jesus, and I will find rest in Jesus's name. Amen.

Praise Break

The mind is what directs the paths of a man. The mind thinks good things and bad things. Through the renewing of the mind with the help of the Holy spirit, restoration is available to all. Restoration of the mind is a beautiful thing. Once you are free from thoughts that have kept you bound, God is able to come in and give clear direction and provide the answers that you desire.

Many who have dealt with mind wars, mental torment, self-sabotage, religious trauma, depression, thoughts of rage, and murder yearn for a peace of mind and for God to deliver them. Psalm 139:23-24 says "search me, O God, and know my heart! Try me and know my thoughts! And see if there is any grievous way in me and lead me in the way everlasting!"

I command this day to be a day of reckoning and transformation of the mind for you. I pray that your heart and mind will be open to how God heals and restore your mind as he has done the same for me. He is no respecter of person, and he loves all his children. There is freedom in God. Reach up and grab it today.

Reflections

-7-

Premature Death

Premature Death has no place in my heart and mind. I declare I will live and not die. Premature death will not choke out my destiny, purpose, or relationship with my heavenly father. I come out of agreement with every illegal contract that was made in secrecy and knowingly. I have been bought with a price and I have purpose in the earth. I shall fulfill the purpose over my life and submit to God in every way. I believe life and death are in the power of the tongue according to Proverbs 18:21. Infirmity, homicide, thoughts of suicide, addictions, depression, premeditation, and trauma bonding will no longer compromise the calling that is over my life. I choose to let go of the past hurt, pain, unforgiveness and bitterness that causes me to choose death. I pull down the strong man of defeat, insecurities, anger, fear, rage, jealously, compromise, comparison, and self-sabotage. I believe in your word that says The Lord will keep me from all harm and you will watch over my life; the Lord will watch over my coming and going both now and forever more according to Psalm 121:7-8. You are my shepherd and protection and I decree that God alone is my refuge, my place of safety and I trust in you according to Psalm 91:1. I believe that those who dwell in the shelter of the highest will abide in the shadow of the Almighty. You will cover me with your feathers and shelter me with your wings. I know I will live a long life according to Psalm 91:16 "With a long life I will satisfy him and let him see my salvation. In Jesus' name. Amen.

Praise Break

Society deems premature death or premature mortality as a death that occurs before the expected age of death in a given population. Many have felt as if they were dying before their time because of the tragedy that has taken place in their life. But God!

I decree and declare that you shall live to the expected end, and nothing shall take you away from the path God has designed specifically for you. I pray God heal the places of fear of dying due to grief and pain of losing a loved one. The word of God says in Jeremiah 29:11, "For I know the plans I have for you," declares the Lord, "plans to prosper you and not to harm you, plans to give you hope and a future." It's not over for you!

My decree is that God will resuscitate you back into the right standing with him. May his presence fill you up and breathe life into you. May every sacrifice, prayer, supplication, and petition unto God not be in vain. I praise God in advance for answering this prayer and continuing to breathe the breath of life into us each day. We serve an awesome God!

Reflections

Breakthrough

ALLISON FOSTER

I am the foster child of the Foster Family. From the womb, I was rejected and neglected. I was the last child, and I wasn't given a middle name, nor was I baptized like my siblings were. I was abused and treated as an outcast by my own bloodline. My toxic parents and childhood trauma caused me not to believe in God or have a relationship with God. This also caused me to never want to have kids of my own.

In March 2012, I became pregnant with my first child. It was a surprise and a total shock. The child's father repeated his generational curse of cheating and ghosting. I was judged by friends and family for getting pregnant before marriage and judged for wanting an abortion. I asked God, "Why is this happening to me?" I never wanted kids, nor did I think I could have kids. I was so depressed and suicidal the entire pregnancy. I lost my job and car during this time. I felt so hopeless. I did not realize at the time but having my son was a blessing, not a curse. Because I suffered from postpartum depression, my son didn't always live with me. Without realizing it, I was passing generational hurt and trauma along to my son.

I became very defensive, isolated, and cold-hearted because of how people were treating me. People pretended to help me but were really trying to control me. My family offered to help just to throw it up in my face later when they were upset. Jezebel and Octopus spirits surrounded me. As time went on, my son moved back in with me and I had a daughter. Life was very up and down. I was wandering as an orphan spirit; therefore, my kids were orphan spirits as well.

When my parents passed away an emotional weight was lifted. Shortly afterwards, familiar spirits tried to control me and my son from the afterlife. My son's behavior was out of control and unexplainable. I honestly wanted to give him away. Therapy wasn't working. Medication wasn't working. My son and I both shared a murderous spirit, and a spirit of rage and suicide. Little did I know this was all planned by the enemy.

In October of 2022 I told my friend Pastor Latoya Christman that I was honestly tired of life and tired of living. She invited me to her church Rebirth Apostolic Ministries. I wasn't going to go at first. When I went the Apostle gave me a deliverance. I felt a change, but I wasn't really ready to commit to the process. I was still drinking, holding grudges, talking to mediums, entertaining toxic people from my past, and not paying my tithes. I still felt like God cursed me with having kids and having to raise them by myself.

June 2023 I was forced to be homeless for 6 months. A former friend and family member put witchcraft and financial hexes on me because I no longer wanted to be around them. This was the worst time of my life. I wasn't listening when God was trying to talk to me. Mentally and spiritually, I struggled for months. The Apostle called me out of nowhere and said, "Daughter come back to church." The kids and I were baptized for the first time on October 27, 2023. That was a spiritual milestone for me. A month later I was blessed with a place for me and the kids.

In January 2024, I decided to isolate, fast, and incorporate daily prayer. During those two months my life changed drastically. My mind and heart feel lighter. I have a better relationship with my kids. I can talk about devastating things that happened to me without getting angry or depressed. I can release relationships and friendships without animosity. I stopped drinking alcohol.

Prayer life changes everything. Having a relationship with God changes everything. My only regret was not building a relationship with God sooner. I am forever thankful to my "Christian Friend," Pastor Latoya Christman. God places certain people in your life for lesson and a blessing.

-8-

Abandonment

Heavenly Father, I come to you now, thanking you for who you are. I lift you up on today, God, and I magnify you. I thank you that today abandonment is no longer a part of who I am. I thank you that the Holy Spirit is my comforter according to John 14:16. So, this too is who I depend on. Father God, I believe by faith that I am more than a conquer through Christ Jesus. I will not be defeated. I will not be crushed. I will not feel rejected, and I am not abandoned. I am a royal priesthood. I believe what your word says in Revelations 21:4 that God will wipe away all depression in the name of Jesus, so I believe by faith that I am holding on to hope according to Romans 4:18:22 even when there were moments when I felt there was no reason to have hope. I thank you even more that you are there for me when I feel crushed in spirit, according to Psalms 34:18. I am a child of God, and I will act as such. I was created in your image, so you have given me the power and authority to be bold as a lion according to Proverbs 28:1. When the world rejected me as the world did unto you, it was counted as an honor, and I count it all as joy in Jesus' name.

Praise Break

Growing up as a child I never really understood the affects abandonment would have on me in my adult years and how much it would affect me mentally, spiritually, and emotionally. Now that I have become an adult, I recognize that even in moments where I felt empty, God was there to comfort me. Abandonment makes a person feel as if no one cares, everyone they love will one day leave or no one is there for them.

Throughout the 40 years of my journey, God has always had his angels to protect, lead and guide me. As I reflect on life, I realize that a lot of times God will allow man to abandon us so that we can draw closer to him and grow intimacy with the father. It is necessary to spend time with the father for intimacy to be built with him. To draw close to him is to be intimate with him.

I no longer sit and think about who abandoned me, rejected me, didn't show up, made me feel less than or who left me when I needed them the most. Instead, I choose to focus on the true, living God who has always been there for me and will continue to be there. He promised to never leave or forsake me and I am standing on His promises. You should, too, because He is worthy, and He has more in store for you. All glory and honor to God. May he bless and keep you.

Reflections

-9-

Abuse

Father, I come to you with an open heart to release and let go of all shame, guilt, condemnation, fear, anxiety and even guilt and lay it at your feet. I acknowledge that you are Yahweh and my healer. I come out of agreement with every soul tie that was created mentally, spiritually, emotionally, and physically with my abuser and the mental wars that continue to cycle throughout my mind. I cancel the assignment of the enemy and every word curse that was spoken against my life by my abuser. I decree and declare by faith every memory of abuse will be eradicated and dismantled by the power of God from my mind. I will no longer allow myself to compromise who you have called me to be. I will no longer entangle myself in relationships and circumstances that will cause mental, emotional, and physical abuse. Forgive me God if I have ever been the abuser towards anyone knowing or unknowingly. Wash me clean with the blood of Jesus for you have called me to a life of righteousness. I will walk in the spirit of righteousness, according to your word. I will no longer allow childhood trauma and abuse to keep me bound, despondent or fruitless. I choose to forgive my abuser and every person who has abused me knowingly and unknowingly. I ask, Oh God, that you will forgive them. I decree and declare that the abuse does not define who I am. I am set free in Jesus' name. I am walking in a new identity because I know who I am. I am not cast away, looked down on, or forgotten. My abuse does not define who I am. I am more than a conqueror through Christ Jesus according to your word in

Romans 8:37. Amen.

Praise Break

Abuse has no place or no future in our lives. When we have crossed over into sonship, we are no longer operating in the old. When we have identified ourselves with Jesus Christ, we now have access to the blessings and the opportunities freely given to us. The hurt and the pain that was caused by our abusers is no longer our responsibility to carry. We know that God has so much more in store for our lives.

Recycling the past or current hurt and trauma will keep us stagnant and unable to fulfill our God-given assignments in the earth. Society encourages us to keep it a secret – to never express or tell others our testimony because of embarrassment. Our testimonies and our truths will set many people free. Someone needs to hear our stories of survival.

Praise God that we don't have to walk in shame. We don't have to walk in condemnation. We are set free and that is why we will go forward in Jesu' name and be all that God has called us to be.

Reflections

-10-

Addictions

Father God, I thank you for the opportunity to come into your presence once again. I thank you that today is a new start to a new beginning in my life. Addictions have controlled my life, and I am ready to release every toxic cycle of addiction. I have escaped my hurt, pain, depression, and trauma. I will no longer allow addictions to run my life or cause me to compromise who I am. I renounce and denounce every alcoholic, perverted, drug use, and reckless behavior that has caused my life to come to stagnancy. I am not defined by my addictions and by faith, I place my struggles at your feet. I thank you God that you are making me clean and whole even in this moment. I decree and declare during moments of struggle and suffering, that I will count it all joy when I meet trials and various kinds for I know that the testing of my faith produces endurance according to James 1:2-4. I trust and totally depend on you for healing and deliverance. Father God, remove every temptation. Every roadblock and every hindrance that causes me to go into cycles of addiction. Remove every relationship that is not meant for me, Father God. Bring people into my life that can assist and help me through my journey to recovery. Allow me to know, oh God, that I do not have to do this alone and that you are there with me and you have provided me with every resource to get the help that I need. Father God, fill up my areas of emptiness. Heal the broken places of my soul. Allow me to see the light at the end of the tunnel. Allow me to know, oh God, that I am not a failure, that I am not incompetent, but I am a survivor in

Jesus's name.

Praise Break

Praise God for relatable people in His word. There is a character in the Bible who struggled with an addiction and his name is Noah. Noah was considered a drunk. Yet, it was Noah's family that God preserved when He flooded the earth. That is an example of the unconditional love of God.

Overindulgence in alcohol may not be your addiction, but at some point, in time you were addicted to something. God makes no mistakes and even in the moments of addictions, the Lord shows his kindness upon all of us. This is why I love to praise Him.

Your story may not be my story, but we all have a story. Never feel like you are the only one that is struggling to get free because you're not. There are many people who struggle in silence and will never speak out or ask for help. But God provides everything you need to break free of your addiction. Grabbing this book and taking your concerns to the Lord in prayer is taking the first step towards deliverance and seeking God's help in this season of your life. \

Because Father God allows us to cast our cares on Him, we have victory over all addictions. Keep pushing and praising. Do not give up on yourself or God. There is someone out there waiting on you to show up and help them along the way to recovery.

Reflections

-11-

Trauma

In Jesus' name I decree and declare I am healed from acute, physical, and emotional trauma that has caused a malfunction in how I treat myself and others. I will no longer allow trauma bonding and toxic relationships or trauma reactions to keep me in cycles. I declare by faith I am healed from every traumatic memory that has caused me to not enjoy life and those who God has sent to be a blessing to my life. I choose to forgive every person who has contributed to the trauma, and I release them now in the name of Jesus. I put on the mindset of Christ according to 1 Corinthians 2:5 that states so that your faith might not rest on human wisdom, but on God's power. I will rely on God's power. I will no longer allow my trauma to tear my family, finances, relationships, ministry partnerships, my place of employment, my marriage, and my children into pieces. I am not what I have gone through, but I am a survivor. I declare trauma will no longer operate through my words, actions, or deeds. I am trauma-free and have been washed with the blood of Jesus. I renounce and denounce every physical, emotional, and psychological verbiage used to tear others down to God. I decree and declare that I am made whole, that I am new in Christ Jesus. I have put off the old self and put on the new self. The new self that is filled with virtue, identity, and substance. I will no longer be afraid to love or receive love. I will put my trust in you, Oh God, that you will never leave me or forsake me in Jesus' name. Amen.

Praise Break

PTSD, formerly known as Post Traumatic Stress disorder, is defined as a person who has difficulty recovering after experiencing or witnessing a terrifying event. The condition can last for months or even years. This disorder is prevalent in today's society. Many suffer from PTSD. Trauma is real but so is God.

I thank God that it will not take months or years for Him to restore, renew and work a miracle in your life. Overcoming traumatic situations and events can be a lot for many to overcome but with the support of friends, family, and God, I believe by faith God will restore your life. I encourage you to speak life no matter what things may look like, or even appear to be. You can praise Him in advance because God will come in and set you free from every traumatic event that has taken place in your life. Trauma does not have to define who you are, and you have the right to be free, you just must believe.

Reflections

-12-

Shame

Father God, I come to you as humbly as I know how thanking you, God, for who you are, and all that you continue to do in my life. I rejoice with praise in my heart for another opportunity to be able to decree and declare that shame will no longer rule or abide in my heart. I thank God that even through mistakes, heart breaks, rejection, being misunderstood and devalued, you saw fit to heal me and deliver me from shame. I believe what your word says in Isaiah 61:7 which states instead of your shame, you shall have double honor, and instead of confusion, they shall rejoice in their portion. I thank you that through the heartbreaks and disappointments you saw fit for me to have double honor in this season. Freedom is my portion and I walk in authority and boldness. Your word is true and living and I come into agreement with second Corinthians 5:17 which states we are new creations in Christ. I do not have to carry shame with me. I acknowledge what your word says in Romans 5:1-5, "Therefore, since we have been justified through faith, we have peace with God through our Lord Jesus Christ, through whom we have also gained access by faith into this grace in which we now stand. And we rejoice in the hope of the glory of God. Not only so, but we also rejoice in our suffering, knowing that suffering produces endurance; endurance produces character, and character produces hope, and hope does not put us to shame because God's love has been poured into our hearts through the Holy Spirit, who has been given to us." I thank you even now for dying on the cross for my sins. I rejoice in my suffering because I understand that even through this moment you are producing something greater within me. I come against the spirit of escape that causes me to hide from the shame and guilt I felt. Isolation and separating myself from people will no longer rule my life. I forgive myself for self-inflicting pain because I did not know my self-worth and the redemptive blood that saves. I choose to forgive people who have spoken words that made me believe I was worthless and not worthy of healing. I commit my mind to Christ and trust in the will and purpose God has for my life. I renounce the spirit of shame that is penetrating through my blood line and cancel every assignment of the enemy, who wants to see me revert backwards into a place of condemnation. I pick up boldness, confidence, and a righteous way of living in Jesus' name. Amen.

Praise Break

Shame as a silent killer that creeps up in moments when we feel like we have fallen short of what God has called us to be. Shame is a tactic used by the enemy so we will forfeit our assignments, but Jesus died to erase all shame. We are restored and renewed through our relationship with almighty God. Because we serve Him our identity, which is true Sonship, is not marred by guilt or shame.

Shame is a destiny killer, a timewaster. Praise God that it will not have dominion over us, By the power and authority given to us by our Father in heaven, we are able to break free from the shackles of shame and the strongholds in the mind that says we not good enough to get that job, have children, get married, become that entrepreneur or even birth our own ministry. We magnify God today because in Him there is freedom and liberty, and we can choose to be set free in Jesus' name.

Reflections

-13-

Angry

A gentle answer deflects anger, but harsh words make tempers flare. (Proverbs 15:1) I thank you, God, that my lips will give forth a gentle answer. I am encouraged today that I no longer walk with resentment in my heart towards your people. I understand that anger can lead to murder and anger leads to evil actions according to Psalms 37:8. I will practice the fruits of the spirit, which are self-control, love, peace, joy, goodness, long suffering, patience, kindness, and gentleness according to Galatians 5:22-23. I understand that self-control considers me a wise man and not a foolish man for your word says in Ecclesiastes 7:9 that we are to control our temper for anger, labels, you a fool. I thank you, God, for you have set a guard around my lips and around my mouth so that I will not speak from a wounded, broken place. I thank you that only wisdom and words that are acceptable unto you will flow out of my mouth. God, I asked that you forgive me for anything that I may have said or done, that may have caused myself or others to forfeit their God-given assignment in the Earth. I come against every word curse that I have spoken over people's lives, being careless with my tongue and my words. I thank you, God, that you are healing my heart, my mind, my soul, and my spirit from any built up angry and resentment that I have towards those who have rejected me and/or betrayed me. I declare in this season that I am drawing close to you. I am building intimacy with you, Father, as I resist the devil and flee from situations or circumstances that will cause me to be triggered or even angry on today. Father God, come in and arrest every faulty system that I have set up because I was angry. I no longer come into agreement with the spirit of offense, rage, and anger that has caused me to want to retaliate and seek revenge against my accusers. I know who I am in you, God. Father, I understand that I am not able to receive the full blessings and favor that is upon my life with anger and bitterness in my heart, so I choose today to renounce and come out of agreement with every open door and entry point I opened for anger to come in. I choose joy today. I choose happiness, long life, fulfillment, excitement, love, forgiveness, and the outpouring of your Holy Spirit in Jesus' name. Amen.

Praise Break

If in the past I could write a book about anger, the title of the book would be my name. Anger is something that I dealt with for many years, and I allowed anger to destroy my relationships with men, my family, friendships, in ministry, as well as, with my daughter for a season. The awesome thing about my healing process is that God is a God who will heal and restore things that we break while in the place of brokenness. I thank God for the joy and the peace that He will give each reader who will come across the prayer that I prayed. I praise Him in advance for giving each of you the encouragement needed to break free from anger. I glorify Him because we do not have to walk around angry, frustrated, or agitated. When we open our hearts to God and tell him what has hurt us deeply and cry out to him, we can choose to be happy, and to have joy in your heart. Overcoming anger is not easy, but it's achievable. When we decide to be intentional about healing and trusting Him, God will reward us with peace, clarity, and happiness moving forward.

Reflections

-14-

Pride

Father God, I honor you for who you are in my life, and I give you the praise, the glory, and the honor. I acknowledge that I cannot do this without you. I have a desire to please you and become one with you, heavenly Father. I understand that pride cannot reside in my life as I advance in my career, marriage, finances, my relationships, and even partnerships in ministry. I humbly accept a new way of living and becoming in this season. I renounce the need to defend myself, be offended, perfectionism, stubbornness, self-reliance, and selfishness because I have allowed pride to take the driver's seat to my life. I understand what your word means when it says pride comes before the fall in Proverbs 16:18. I chose to be a generational curse breaker and the stronghold of pride will no longer run my emotions, thoughts, or feelings. I will not bring disgrace to myself due to pride according to Proverbs 11:2. I come to you, Father in prayer as a humble servant asking you to search my heart and reveal the areas where I have allowed pride to take over, praying that you will guide me with the help of the Holy Spirit to remove pride from my life. I believe by faith all things are possible for those who believe. I believe on today in Jesus' name. Amen.

Praise Break

I can rejoice in the fact that I am still alive. Pride once kept me from obtaining my place in the kingdom of God, it was an unwelcome guest in every fiber of my being. It took up residence in my heart, mind, and soul. I was unaware of just how bound I was by pride. Then I came into the knowledge of God and began to seek Him. I was convicted in my spirit, and I began to take inventory of everything that had taken root in me that was not pleasing to the Father. I found things that were not obvious to the naked eye but were visible with the discerning of spirits. I uncovered that pride, and the Lord God delivered me from it. Because I want to mirror the life of Christ, there is no room for pride to dwell. By the grace of God, I am able to live a life of humility, serving Him with gladness. The one thing I can be proud of is my relationship with God. He calls me friend! (John 15:15)

Reflections

Breakthrough

CAROL FIELDS

The worst time in my life, the time when I was most depressed, was when my kids were taken from me and put into foster care. At the time I was living in a shelter and still under the influence of drugs and alcohol. The name of the shelter and church was Bible of Tabernacle. It was located in Venice, California.

One day I felt like I needed a break – just to get away and find time alone. So, there was a woman at the shelter who was much older than me. I trusted to watch my two kids. I paid her to babysit. I just wanted some quiet time, but little did I know, she was an alcoholic also. She left my kids all alone. When I came back, my kids were gone. I had just missed them by ten minutes. I looked to see where they were, and they were in the back seat of a police car. This was the worst day of my life. I just wanted to die.

I blamed myself for many years. I felt less than a woman and a mom. I went to court on every court date again and again, and nobody showed up to support me. So, I asked the court what I needed to do to get my kids back. I did what they asked of me, but it was not good enough. I never got them back. For many years I struggled with drug use. I moved out of the city and continued to use more drugs and they took over my life. I felt like I was not good enough to live because I never got my kids back. So, I went even deeper into a depression.

I just got tired of life. I really did not want to live anymore, and I attempted to commit suicide. I really did not want to die but depression took over me at the time. I was put in a mental hospital where I tried to overdose. I already had PCP in my system, and I flipped out. When I was in the mental hospital, I knew that I was not supposed to be there, and I fought my way out. I talked with counselors. I investigated a church home so I could start living again. I held on to my counseling and my faith in God.

There were times when I felt all alone. No one could fill the void that I felt but God. All of this took place between the years 1985 and 1998. I kept on talking to God, praying for the strength to hold on. I am currently working through my sobriety. I have my own place and am taking medication to help me through. I go to women’s shelters from time to time to encourage and support the women, but the ultimate gift is my relationship with God.

I currently reside in Houston, Texas, where I'm close to three of my five children. I lost one child in 2006 to gang violence and my other child still lives in California. I am now able to see my grandchildren and experience their lives and communicate with my children often. I give God the glory, the praise, and the honor. and I encourage those around me. If I can make it out of depression, anybody can.

-15-

Perversion

Father God, you are the healer and sustainer of my faith. I decree and declare that by faith I am delivered and set free from the spirit of perversion. I understand the stronghold of perversion is something that must be broken off my life for me to walk in purity and holiness. I believe what your word says in Galatians 5:24-25, which says those who belong to Christ Jesus have nailed the passions and desires of their sinful nature to His cross and crucified them there. Since we are living by the Spirit, let us follow the spirits lead in every part of our lives. I trust that by faith I am allowing the Holy Spirit to lead my life and I choose to relinquish every desire that does not please you. I will try to live in peace with everyone and to be holy because without holiness no one will see the Lord according to Hebrews 12:14. I thank God For the renewing, the refreshing, and the purging that you will continue to do in me and through me. I open my heart, mind, and spirit to purification. I believe what your word says in Romans 6:22, "but now that you have been set free from sin and have become slaves of God, the benefits you reap leads to holiness, and the result is eternal life." I thank you God that I live a disciplined life that will not contaminate my body, my spirit, or my mind. I choose to connect with others who will not contaminate my process towards purification. I thank you, God, for rescuing me from the hands of the enemy. I understand I am a new self, created to be like God in true righteousness and holiness according to Ephesians 4:24.

Praise Break

When the enemy comes in like a flood, The Spirit of the Lord will lift up a standard against him. (Isaiah 59:19) Perversion came to kill my destiny, but God! Perversion had me bound for many seasons, but God! Perversion caused me to be stagnant and I was not able to move toward fulfilling my God-given destiny, but God!. Perversion took root in the heart and tried to kill the fruits of the Spirit, but God! The wonderful thing about living this life as a believer is that we serve a gracious, loving God. When others judged, He came in and cleaned up. God showed love and compassion towards me while I was yet a sinner. I am continually in a place of humility, reverence, and honor towards God. It is an ultimate blessing to be in the household of faith, to worship God, to praise God just because of who he is. His grace and mercy are everlasting and sufficient, not only for me, but also for you. Today, don't worry about what you may have done in your past or your current struggle. Know that God is with you and giving up is never an option. Keep pressing and keep pushing towards holiness. One day you will wake up and see yourself as a new person. To God be the glory!

Reflections

-16-

Self-Sabotage

I cry out to you father with thanksgiving, praise, and worship. My heart says thank you. Thank you for your love, your grace, and your mercy. I thank you God that in moments of self-sabotage you saw fit to show me your glory, your favor, and your love. Father, I recognize your blood that was shed on the cross for the remission of sins so that I may have life and have it more abundantly. I come against every assignment of the enemy that causes me to sabotage relationships, job opportunities, ministry growth and expansion, as well as the ability to see the gifts and talents that you have placed on the inside of me. I come out of agreement with every word curse I spoke about myself and to myself that killed my dreams, business opportunities, wealth, and destiny. I thank you for what your word says, according to John 3:16 "For God so loved the world, that he gave his only Son, that whoever believes in him should not perish but have eternal life." You sacrificed your son so that I may have life and I thank you. Father God, you loved me enough to see the good in me, the purpose you created, and the beauty in your creation. I renounce every lie told to me that caused me to doubt the plan you have for my life and my generation to come. I understand my words are powerful and the posture of my heart matters. I will no longer defile my destiny or speak words that will alter the plans you have for me. I understand what the word says in Mark 7:20-23: "It is what comes from inside that defiles you." And I will move forward knowing I have power over my words. I will be great. I will be awesome. I will make something out of my life and go after every dream and failed attempt. I understand that I can do all things through Christ who strengthens me, and I walk boldly proclaiming my victory over the enemy in Jesus' name Amen.

Praise Break

I have observed over the years how self-sabotage destroyed people's lives and as a result, they aborted their destiny and every plan that God put in place for their lives. The awesome thing that I love so much about God is He is a God of second chances. Through repentance, when we are open, honest, and transparent, God is able to come in and heal the places of our hearts and our soul that are empty. Our Father knows exactly what we need and when we need. He will place someone in our path to encourage, inspire and uplift us so we can get to our next place in Him.. I have had moments when self-sabotage stunted my growth because I believed what the enemy said concerning my life instead of what God promised over my life. I'm here to encourage you today. By the grace of God, every plan, every dream, business idea, and desire for your life will come to pass. Put forth the effort. Be diligent. Be faithful. Trust and believe in what the Word of God is saying over for your life, and you will come out on the other end victorious. Be blessed!

Reflections

-17-

Finances

Father God, I lift you. I praise your name for you are the true living God. I thank you for being my provider and sustainer. I thank you for keeping me mentally, spiritually, and financially while I was being irresponsible with my finances. I decree and declare on this day I will plan, create, execute, and build financial wealth for me and my family. I will no longer walk in lack or believe the lies of the enemy concerning my finances. I will build partnerships, business ideas, and relationships with people who will help get me to the place to which God has called me. I will be responsible for my finances and budget my money with the knowledge and information given by partnerships, and trusted referrals. I will no longer walk in fear of not having enough because the word of God states in 1 Timothy 6:10-11: "For the love of money is the root of all kinds of evil. And some people, craving money, have wandered from the true faith and pierced themselves with many sorrows. But you, Timothy, are a man of God; so, run from all these evil things. Pursue righteousness and a godly life, along with faith, love, perseverance, and gentleness." I shall pursue righteousness. I will understand the meaning of money management and God's provision for I trust in you. I will not wander from my faith craving money and making it as an idol. God as your word says in Jeremiah 17:7-8: "But blessed are those who trust in the Lord and have made the Lord their hope and confidence." I will put my trust and hope in you, Lord. "They are like trees planted along a riverbank, with roots that reach deep into the water. Such trees are not bothered by the heat or worried by long months of drought. Their leaves stay green, and they never stop producing fruit." I decree and declare I will never stop producing fruit. I will be responsible, and I can be trusted in Jesus's name. Amen.

Praise Break

There was a time when I did not understand the value of money or the responsibility that is attached to God blessing us with an abundance. I remember moments when I did not have enough money to pay for things for me and my child and feeling anxious, fearful of lack, worry, and desperation. During these times, I had to build faith and learn to totally depend on God and trust that He would provide for me. I really did not know what dependence looked like or how it worked, but because I had no choice but to trust, God showed up and provided. I remember praising and thanking God for blessing me and making ways. I did not give man the credit but God. Trusting God is easier said than done but the reward in the end is so much greater than we can ever think or imagine. I thank God for tearing down my old mindset and placing people like Apostle Shantay Ligons to teach me sound doctrine so that I would tithe and be blessed by my obedience. I praise God for wisdom, knowledge, and understanding and a closer walk with Him. I encourage you to trust that God will increase your finances in Jesus' name because you cannot beat God's giving.

Reflections

-18-

Ministry

Father God, I acknowledge your grace and mercy. I am redeemed by the blood of the lamb because of Christ blood shed on Calvary. I repent for neglecting the call to my life and rebelling against what you have instructed me to do in the earth. I am an overcomer, and I shall act and speak as such. I have been called to build the kingdom and I will not retract the mandate over my life for You have called me to the great commission and to be a disciple for the Lord. I declare I will walk in servanthood, humility, the fruits of the spirit and boldness for the kingdom. I will not look at ministry as a part of what I do but who I am. Everything about who I am identifies as work unto the Lord. I will take on the mind of Christ and suffer as he suffered to do the work of the Lord. I will no longer doubt my calling, my position, or my identity. You have created me in your image, God. I will lead the people of God with enthusiasm as your word says in Romans 12:11-12 "Never be lazy but work hard and serve the Lord enthusiastically. I will not complain, murmur, rebel, or talk my way out of the assignment that you have called me to. My heart posture in ministry will be one of clean hands and a pure heart. I forgive past and present broken promises from ministry relationships. I release every false expectation I placed on people. I release them now from guilt and condemnation. I will no longer hold on to bitterness, anger, resentment, or unforgiveness towards people who have hurt me or mishandled the calling that is on my life. I choose to let the pain go. I will no longer rehash conversations and dialogues with people who have lied or betrayed my trust. I take captive my thoughts and I decree and declare I am healed and set free, I choose to walk in freedom and liberty from this day forward in Jesus' name. Amen.

Praise Break

I have heard the term "church hurt" used several times. There are many people who self-identify with these words and as a result, stop responding to the call that is on their life because of people. I, too, was a person who felt the rejection and pain from those in ministry, but when I realized my assignment and purpose had nothing to do with what people had done or said about me, I gained the confidence I needed to thrive. I sought the healing that was needed, the confidence through the Word of God, and the right teaching and leader that would cultivate and guide me to the place where God had called me. It had everything to do with timing and my yielding to the calling. The mandate and calling that is upon my life was greater than what I was experiencing. He has called me to the rejected and the abandoned. Sometimes the very thing that has hurt us is the very thing to which we are called. I pray that you will find refuge and peace in knowing that God has called you to something bigger and greater beyond the hurt, pain, and rejection in Jesus' name. I give God all the glory for bringing me out of "church hurt."

Reflections

-19-

Anxiety

Father God, I lift you up and I magnify you, oh God, I give you the praise, the glory, and the honor for who you are. Father, I decree and declare on this day that I will no longer walk in anxiety, I renounce and denounce every word curse or generational curse on my bloodline of anxiety. I come out of agreement with every faulty system that has been set up that has caused me to be anxious for nothing. I decree anxiety has no place in my heart, emotions, decision making, or in my interaction with people. Anxiety has no place in my life, and I give total access for God to be my comforter and peace. I will not be consumed by anxiety for the word says in 1 Peter 5:7 to cast all your anxieties on him, because he cares for you. I cast my cares on the Lord today. This burden is too heavy for me to carry, and I need you, God. Anxiety will not run my finances, my mind, or relationships with others. I will create healthy coping skills to help manage my anxiety by reading the word of God and relying on the holy spirit to give me the confidence and reassurance. I will encourage myself and believe in myself. I know that I can do all things through Christ that strengthens me, and I am more than a conquer through Christ Jesus. I release generalized anxiety disorder, obsessive-compulsive disorder, panic disorder, post-traumatic stress disorder, social anxiety disorder, phobias, separation anxiety disorder and agoraphobia that has kept me isolated and stagnant. I will no longer allow anxiety to keep me from fulfilling my purpose on earth. I have confidence, boldness, and support from others to help overcome anxiety. I believe and trust in God that he will give me joy, peace, and happiness in Jesus' name. Amen.

Praise Break.

Anxiety sometimes can feel like an unwelcome guest. If you have operated in anxiety from childhood to adulthood, it becomes a stronghold. Many people struggle with anxiety across the world and for some it feels unbearable. I remember times of feeling anxiety and I just did not know why. It wasn't until I became knowledgeable of the Word of God, and I understood how powerful my words were that I was able to pray and come out of agreement with anxiety. It takes a strong and determined person to no longer allow anxiety to rule their lives. I thank God for giving me the strength to overcome anxiety. My prayer is That you will also find the courage and the strength to walk in boldness and be fearful in Jesus' name.

Reflections

-20-

Suicide

I come with full aggression, with the authority and power of Jesus Christ, to bind the hand of every suicidal thought that has kept me in a repetitive negative thought pattern and that has been a stronghold against my future destiny and purpose. I dismantle and annihilate, by the power of the Holy Ghost, the desire to take my life by way of deception from the enemy. I have a purpose. I have destiny. I am a conqueror. I will not be defeated. I come against every word curse spoken over my life and I cancel the assignment of premature death. I thank you, God, that you have given me a choice to live according to Deuteronomy 30:19-20 "today I have given you the choice between life and death, between blessings and curses. Now I call on heaven and earth to witness the choice you make. All that you would choose life so that you and your descendants might live. You can make this choice by loving the Lord your God, obeying him, and committing yourself firmly to him. This is a key to your life." I thank you, oh God, for the option to choose life on today. God, I choose your love and I open my heart to you. I put on the mind of Christ and the helmet of salvation. I come against mood-altering substances that plague my thoughts and keep me confused, angry, rejected, unworthy, grieved, condemned and lifeless. I will not allow suicide to be the cry of my mother or father. There is nothing too big for God, so I trust in him. I am better than what others have said about me because I am a child of God. I have been created to do the work of the Lord and it will be fulfilled on the earth. I choose to live and not die. I will live a long life. I am a walking testimony of what God can do for me and through me in Jesus' name. Amen.

Praise Break

I have seen and witnessed that life or death is in the power of the tongue. I have seen miracles happen and people's lives change forever by ways of faith and belief that living is far better than dying. So many people deal with suicidal thoughts because they feel like life is too much to bear, and things have become so overwhelming that they have no other option but to take their life. We hear countless stories of those who are young and even old who leave this world too soon. It is the enemy's design to keep you in the place of defeat, isolated, feeling alone, as if no one loves you or cares about you, because it is the enemy's goal is to take as many as God's children out of the world prematurely. My prayer is that you will find hope in moments of despair and discomfort. I pray that God will bring someone into your life that will inspire and motivate you to live. Every day will not be easy, and God never promised that it would be, but life and death is in the power of the tongue. When you speak that you shall live, just know the world has no choice but to line up with the commands that has come out of your mouth in Jesus's name.

Reflections

-21-

Depression

Father, I come to you with praise, adoration, and worship in my heart. I thank you for being the God of second chances. I recognize your saving power. I renounce and come out of agreement with depression and the heaviness that has kept me from fulfilling my God-given assignment in the earth. I willfully open my heart to the purpose and plan for my life. I accept what you have said about my life. I bind the hand of identity confusion, self-sabotaging thoughts, fear, anxiousness, loneliness, abandonment, rejection, night terrors, trauma and memories that recycle over and over in my mind that cause me to become depressed. Depression has no place in my mind, will, or emotions. I come against the temptation to use drugs, alcohol, or any other coping mechanism to cope with depression. I am independent of depression and no longer dependent on how I feel or my own ways of thinking. I welcome accountability. I embrace help from others, and I will no longer isolate or withdraw from those who God has sent to love me. I am loved, I am an overcomer, and the joy of the Lord is my strength. I welcome faith and prosperity into my life. I do not have to be a victim of my circumstances or situations. I will no longer sit on the side lines and abandon my kingdom assignment because of depression. I own and accept who God has called me to be and I close the door on everything that has caused stagnation. I will no longer be afraid to face my past, present or future. I am not alone for in Christ Jesus I am made whole and new. I surrender my life to you God. I welcome in the Holy Spirit, and I give full permission for him to rest in my heart. I am bigger than depression. I am bigger than what others have said and thought about me. I am not rejected. “And I am convinced that nothing can ever separate us from God's love. Neither death nor life, neither angels nor demons, neither our fears for today nor our worries about tomorrow. Not even the powers of hell can separate us from God's love” According to Romans 8:38-39. In Jesus’ name. Amen.

Praise Break

There are no words to describe God's grace and unconditional love. Even in moments when we did not love ourselves, God loved us. Moments when we felt like throwing in the towel and giving up because depression had us so weighed down, God sent his holy spirit as a comforter. I encourage those who read this entire journal to know that you did not make it this far to give up now. He never told us that the road would be easy, but I don't believe He brought you this far to leave you. The fight and perseverance to keep going is what he desires from all of us. This is what gives us hope and a new zeal to keep going. I encourage you to go back and reread the prayers and praise breaks during difficult times in your life. I declare today will be the start of a new beginning in your life. Be blessed!

Reflections

Breakthrough

MINISTER LATOYA CHRISTMAN

It was the year 2013 when I officially made it back to Houston from Grand Prairie, TX after a split from my ex-husband. The move was not planned; it was totally unexpected. I had to move in with my now deceased foster mother and a four-month-old baby, wondering what was next for my life. I felt empty, numb, betrayed, lied on and in total shock. I dealt with much anger, bitterness, unforgiveness and grief from the loss of my adoptive father. Trying to process so much at once was overwhelming while getting let go from a job I had worked for several years and having to face peers and loved ones. I felt embarrassed and crushed. I had lost so much weight from stress that I didn't recognize myself. In addition, having to lay to rest my foster dad and support his widow was a blur afterwhile. Depression was a silent killer in those moments. I was coping with everyday life while feeling numb and pretending to be sane for the sake of my daughter. As I look back at my life and see where God brought me from, I know that it's nothing but a miracle. I'm a living testimony that if you continue to fight for your life and not allow setbacks to get you off track, God will bring healing to your life in ways that you cannot even imagine. To be in a place now where I am on my third book, operating in my calling, working a job that pays well, living a life of peace and happiness, and my daughter is doing great is so fulfilling. The best advice that I can give anyone who is struggling with depression is to understand that giving up is not an option. If you can put your feet on the ground every day when you get out of the bed and take the first step, God will do the rest. I did this for months and each day got better and better. It is the enemy's plan to kill our destiny in its infant state, but we have the victory in God to overcome. So many lives have been changed, people committed their life to Christ, and walking in their purpose because I came out of a dead season that was meant to kill me. Think about the lives you will save because of overcoming this giant called depression. I am a testimony of what God can do in a person who is struggling to come out of a dark place. I encourage you on today that you can press, push pass, and overcome by faith in Jesus' name.

About the Author

Los Angeles native, Latoya Christman is an author, a mother of one, certified board counselor and Pastor currently residing in Houston, TX. She obtained a bachelor's degree in political science from Bennett College for Women in Greensboro, NC. Christman was featured in Houston Voyage Magazine, and Purposely Awakened News and Media in Southern California. Dismantling the Stronghold of Depression is her third book. Her debut book, "A Hidden Treasure Behind a Wounded Heart," changed lives through the testimony and challenges faced as a child. Her future goal is to become a business owner and work full-time in ministry, which has been her desire. Her hope is to one day see a community of believers operating in their gifts according to God's word.

Made in the USA
Middletown, DE
23 December 2024

66219248R00055